SCENES
of America

ATLANTIC CITY

SCENES
of America
ATLANTIC CITY

JOHN T. CUNNINGHAM AND **KENNETH D. COLE**

Copyright © 2006 by John T. Cunningham and Kenneth D. Cole
ISBN 0-7385-4625-9

Published by Arcadia Publishing
Charleston SC, Chicago IL, Portsmouth NH, San Francisco CA

Library of Congress control number: 2006926837

For all general information contact Arcadia Publishing at:
Telephone 843-853-2070
Fax 843-853-0044
E-mail sales@arcadiapublishing.com
For customer service and orders:
Toll-Free 1-888-313-2665

Visit us on the Internet at www.arcadiapublishing.com

On the cover: Atlantic City's early promoters claimed their beach gave birth to the art of sand sculpture. Masters of the form included James J. Taylor, seen here in 1908 finishing a piece entitled *Song*. (ACFPL.)

CONTENTS

	INTRODUCTION	7
1.	THE EARLY DAYS	9
2.	A NEW CENTURY	35
3.	TIMES OF CHANGE	83
4.	TOWARD THE MODERN ERA	109

INTRODUCTION

The island has been called Atlantic City since 1853, when only 21 registered voters shared the pristine beach with squawking seagulls, horseshoe crabs, and dancing sandpipers. A few visitors rowed across Absecon Bay in summertime to frolic on the dunes.

The first visitors came on July 1, 1854, riding the jolting, dirty cars on the maiden trip of the Camden and Atlantic Railroad. Three days later, the first excursion train made the same round trip; the incoming crowds have never vanished—in summertime, at least.

Boardinghouses rose, followed by small wooden hotels. The first boardwalk, conceived in 1870 and laid directly on the beach, heralded a new day. Several boardwalks have followed, culminating in the modern permanent fixture. In 1882, the first of Atlantic City's famous amusement piers opened, encouraging others to build piers stretching from the boardwalk out into the ocean, in effect increasing the boardwalk's scope.

Huge brick hotels were in place or were being built at the end of the 19th century. Already known as the "Queen of Resorts," the city knew well the three elements that one promoter of the 1950s would call "Ocean, emotion and plenty of promotion."

Atlantic City entrepreneurs believed that the beautiful years would last forever. The rich and the famous strolled the boardwalk in the 1920s. Miss America made her debut in 1921. The huge

Convention Hall opened in 1929. City visitation swelled, and the city reached its prime. Thus, the Great Depression of the 1930s struck with savage intensity.

World War II was a dramatic turning point. German submarines lurking off the coast actually sank about a dozen ships. By 1942, the armed services began taking over boardwalk hotels to house and feed thousands of military personnel. Eventually almost 50 hotels were under military control, and the Convention Center was the armed forces' headquarters.

Atlantic City had fully returned to its prewar status by 1950, attracting huge state and national conventions and millions of regular visitors. The Easter parade flourished. Hotels were filled, although many of the huge, outmoded wooden hotels and boardinghouses were demolished in the 1960s to make room for higher profit-yielding motels.

Today, although it has changed tremendously, Atlantic City may be more mystical than ever. Huge crowds storm the doors of the casinos, as if mere entrance assured good fortune. The old recipe for success has been changed (however unofficially) to "promotion, emotion, and very occasionally, the ocean."

Images from the Heston Collection of the Atlantic City Free Public Library are denoted by the abbreviation "ACFPL." Those from the Miss America Organization collection are noted by "MAO." Those owned by Robert Ruffolo and Princeton Antiques Bookshop are designated "Ruffolo." The images from Conectiv are designated "Conectiv." Images from the Atlantic County Historical Society are designated "ACHS." Images from the personal collection of John T. Cunningham are marked "JTC." All copyrighted images depicting facets of the Miss America pageant are reprinted here with the permission of the Miss America Organization, Atlantic City, New Jersey.

THE EARLY DAYS

Absecon Lighthouse and its keeper's quarters, shown in 1868, were built in the city's Inlet neighborhood in 1867. The lighthouse is the only remaining Atlantic City landmark dating from the city's earliest days. Thanks to the shifting sands of time, it now sits several hundred feet further from the water than when it opened. Originally painted orange and black, the lighthouse was completely restored in 1998–1999 and stands as a reminder of all that Atlantic City has experienced since its founding. (ACFPL.)

Dr. Jonathan Pitney is properly called the "Father of Atlantic City." He had been touting Absecon Island's healthy climate for many years before convincing Camden and Atlantic Railroad entrepreneurs that a beach resort could draw customers via the railroad. The first accommodations for tourists were in "Aunt Millie" Leeds's substantial two-story frame house, opposite. This oldest Atlantic City rooming house was built around 1815. (JTC; opposite, ACFPL.)

Less than 25 years after Atlantic City's first official visitors arrived in July 1854 to spend a day on the nearly deserted beach, this panoramic lithograph, drawn around 1870, shows startling change. Boardinghouses and small hotels line the streets, following the railroad tracks to the sea. Two can be recognized—Schaufler's, on the left center, and the United States Hotel, in the distance on the right. Atlantic City's foremost preoccupation had already come to be keeping guests in town overnight, for a week, a month, or, if possible, the entire season. As the hotels grew increasingly large, most of their interiors became evermore plush. Hotels served as the centers of activity, and customer satisfaction became the hallmark of the city's hotel services. (JTC.)

Schaufler's Hotel and Summer Gardens on North Carolina Avenue, photographed sometime in the 1870s, typified early Atlantic City hotels. It was what might be called basic, with no private baths. At the time, no hotel had a private bath for every guest. Railroad conductors went to the doors of Schaufler's bar to warn passengers that the train for Philadelphia was about to depart. (ACFPL.)

When hotel owners complained in 1870 about the sand that was tracked into their establishments, train conductor Alexander Boardman and hotel keeper Jacob Keim suggested building a wooden walkway atop the beach. By that June, Atlantic City had spent $5,000 on a moveable boardwalk, seen in this 1876 engraving. In the decades ahead, those 12-foot sections of pine planks, only 8–10 feet wide, grew into a business and entertainment legend. (ACFPL.)

The farms of the Garden State fed Atlantic City and its visitors. For decades, all meat, milk, grain, and produce crossed the bay via the railroad. These goods were carted for sale in the open-air market, seen here in 1876. Atlantic City imported everything from the mainland. Even drinking water was brought in until city engineers discovered the Pinelands aquifer 1,500 feet beneath the sand. (ACFPL.)

In Atlantic City around 1880, hotels and boardinghouses had proliferated across the island. In this view, a long train passes the splendid new municipal building and courthouse, recently erected, and heads for the varied hotels and boardinghouses along the right-of-way. (ACHS.)

The city's Sand Pier is shown as it appeared in the August 1885 *Harper's Weekly*. Atlantic City may not have introduced amusement piers to the world, but it made the most of them, including this simple one for fashionable lounging. (Ruffolo.)

Built in 1880, this more permanent boardwalk created a boundary for the business district, and real estate prices skyrocketed. Eventually more than 50 bathhouses (such as Bew's, shown in 1885) leased suits to bathers. Few tourists actually braved the waves any further than knee deep. Few knew how to swim. Besides, Atlantic City's promoters had championed the benefits of sea air, not seawater. (ACFPL.)

The 1887 introduction of rolling chairs added a touch of luxury to the boardwalk. Adapted from wheelchairs, the wicker chairs of Philadelphian Harry Shill earned a place in the Smithsonian. Rolling chairs had their own parade, the Floral Parade, before Miss America festivities subsumed it in 1921. The chairs, however, carried contestants down the boardwalk for decades thereafter. By 1940, some chairs accommodated up to four people, opposite, with two men pedaling. Motorized chairs appeared briefly before being banned in the 1960s. (ACFPL.)

Atlantic City's commercial fishing fleet fed the palates of eastern cities and supplied fare to local establishments. The fleet was headquartered in the marinas of the Northside and Inlet sections, among them the Fenton and Leeds docks, seen here in 1890. Another dock at Gardner's Basin now houses the New Jersey State Marina. (ACFPL.)

Fire was a major enemy in a city built entirely of wood. Fire brigades organized, and the Neptune Hose Company, seen here in 1897, was one of the city's oldest, having been founded in 1882. When they were not sharpening their musical skills, the members fought flames at establishments that subscribed to the company's services. Atlantic City consolidated all its volunteer fire companies into one public department in 1904. (ACFPL.)

A NEW CENTURY

The beach was a full-dress affair, as this family portrait in 1900 attests. Women donned bathing dresses and stockings to sit on the beach, if they changed at all. Men could bare their arms and some of their legs, but the law prevented any greater a display of skin. Non-bathers in the party dressed almost as formally to sit in the sand with their families as to go to work or church. (ACFPL.)

The city's streets were made of sand well into the 20th century, even after electrical and telephone lines had made inroads by 1900. Horses and carriages, like this one outside a restaurant near the intersection of New Jersey and Atlantic Avenues, kept the pace of Atlantic City manageable for decades. (ACFPL.)

Restaurants were a major Atlantic City business. In 1900, the Extra Dry restaurant advertised its imported wines, liquors, and dining parlors for men and women. Such parlors were an important consideration in a time when a woman risked her reputation if she walked the streets unescorted or dined alone. (ACFPL.)

Atlantic City spared no expense in 1904 to celebrate the 50th anniversary of its founding. The city decked out Atlantic Avenue with a colonnade and triumphant arch straddling the trolley tracks near the intersection with South Carolina Avenue. (ACFPL.)

Originally built as the Iron Pier in 1886, Heinz Pier at Massachusetts Avenue, seen in 1905, marketed H. J. Heinz brands for more than 40 years. This was done with exhibits, cooking demonstrations, model interiors, and souvenir pins shaped like pickles. Although located well north of the main business district, it remained a boardwalk mainstay until the hurricane of 1944 damaged it beyond repair. (ACFPL.)

Fishing was and remains one of the most dangerous of occupations. To bring in their catch in 1906, the fishermen of the *Alberta* prepared for the worst that the sea and sky could deliver in a time before weather forecasting. Little is left of the commercial fleet now, but Atlantic City retains a sizable sport-fishing fleet. (ACFPL.)

The Traymore Hotel, old and new, offered a fine comparison of the changing hotel architecture and building size in the city. The Traymore, seen here around 1910, was the very essence of Victorian architecture and elegant aloofness. The new Traymore opened in 1915. It stood 14 stories tall, had 600 guest rooms, and typified the several towering brick palaces erected in the early 20th century. (ACFPL.)

When noted aviator Glenn Curtiss flew over Atlantic City in 1910 in his flimsy single-engine biplane, he came in low over one of the city's newest hotels, the Marlborough-Blenheim Hotel. It was the first hotel in the world built with reinforced concrete. World-famous inventor Thomas A. Edison, who perfected the process of pouring concrete walls for large structures, came often to the city to watch progress. (ACFPL.)

A 1910 storm stranded the *Alpha*, seen here, within feet of the boardwalk, where it became a free Atlantic City attraction. When the brig *Strandet* was beached in the 19th century, its captain had charged admission to tour the wreck. Not until the city began dune restoration in the 1970s did storm-driven flooding in city streets abate to any degree. (ACFPL.)

Despite protests by Atlantic City promoters that "snow never falls on the city," this locomotive had trouble moving along an Atlantic City street during a heavy snowstorm before World War I. It was off-season, of course, so no tourists were involved, and the slow pace disturbed no one. (ACFPL.)

Petite, pert, and just a bit naughty, befitting a young woman of the Roaring Twenties, Margaret Gorman of Washington, D.C., was chosen in 1921 as the first "most beautiful girl in America." Gorman, age 16, wore a loose-fitting, black bathing suit and showed dimpled knees above rolled-down, black stockings. She had to post a $5,000 bond to assure that she would return the trophy, which could be retired by the first woman to win it three times. (JTC.)

OPPOSITE: Style and modesty in 1921 demanded hats. Two brave contestants, defying tradition, showed their bobbed hair. The eight young "beauty maids" represented cities—Washington, Pittsburgh, Newark, New York, Ocean City, Camden, Philadelphia, and Harrisburg. (JTC.)

In the second year of the pageant, 57 girls competed for the privilege of posting a $5,000 bond for the Golden Mermaid, which would be given outright to the first young beauty to win it three times. When Mary Campbell of Columbus, Ohio, won in 1922 and 1923, promoters gave her a replica of the trophy and told her never to compete again. This free boardwalk parade of beauties in 1923 was part of the judging process. The show attracted thousands of spectators. (JTC.)

It was far from frolicking, yet it was at least fraternizing when judges walked the beach with some of the 1923 contestants. Forty years later, this would have been considered a grave breach of protocol. When a new and stronger group of promoters took hold in 1940, rules became strict, and chaperones were close by when candidates for the crown appeared anywhere in public. (MAO.)

Miss Philadelphia, Ruth Malcolmson, gathered her court of other beauties in 1924 for a photograph after she was chosen Miss America. The setting must have delighted the promoters. Here were several of the nation's most beautiful women sitting in wicker chairs as serenely and as elegantly as if they were West Philadelphian newlyweds meeting for afternoon tea rather than contestants in a national "beauty show." (MAO.)

He bore not the slightest resemblance to Bert Parks, who in future days would rule supreme in the crowning of Miss America, but in 1926, King Neptune was acceptable at the coronation. Here, he crowns Norma Smallwood, who took the coveted headpiece back to her home town of Tulsa, Oklahoma. (MAO.)

Businesses in 1900 advertised heavily. The competition for attention was so intense that outlandish promotion became an Atlantic City hallmark. For example, film star W. C. Fields started in Atlantic City as a juggler; between acts, however, he was paid to pretend to drown near Fortescue's Pier. The mock rescues, as many as 12 per day, attracted crowds to the pier. Atlantic City promoted itself, too. The annual Easter parade, as shown here in 1930, was started in 1876 to stem the loss of visitors to Philadelphia's Centennial Exposition. Although New York City had an older event, Atlantic City offered prizes and attracted crowds of up to 500,000. Rain, shine, or snow, it has been held every year since. (ACFPL.)

The Atlantic City Beach Patrol was always close to the hearts of city leaders. Technically speaking, the Atlantic City Beach Patrol was integrated. However, its African American members were usually consigned, as were all black bathers, to a patch of sand derisively called Chicken Bone Beach. Located at Missouri Avenue, Chicken Bone Beach became a New Jersey state landmark in 1997. One of its patrols in the 1930s stands in front of George Walls's bathhouse. (ACFPL.)

From the sea, Convention Hall looks like the world's biggest Quonset hut, but there was never a Quonset structure to rival this. It stretches from the boardwalk to Atlantic Avenue and between Georgia and Mississippi Avenues. It occupies seven acres of some of the most valuable real estate in the world. The city's public relations people long have contended that it is the "world's most famous auditorium." It has been the nation's meeting place for years—the place where teachers, doctors, lawyers, scientists, politicians, automobile salesmen, municipal workers, and hundreds of other groups convened. (ACFPL.)

Sports are an important part of Convention Hall activities. This jousting meet in 1932 was the first indoor surface to permit horses in an indoor jousting tournament. (ACFPL.)

Several times a day between 1929 and 1978, young women in swimsuits coaxed trained horses off a 40-foot tower into 12 feet of water, as seen here in 1933. Although it originated in the Midwest, the diving horse act made the Steel Pier the most famous amusement pier in the world. Neither horses nor riders suffered serious injuries, and few other acts attracted larger crowds. (ACFPL.)

Every imaginable act played the piers. Some of them included the human cannonball (here in 1935), boxing cats, skiing dogs, and reenactments of the Johnstown flood or the destruction of Pompeii. Broadway musicals tested their material in local theaters, and "anthropological" exhibits from the Pacific Islands—with islanders living in grass huts—enticed visitors to the boardwalk. (ACFPL.)

The ice business was lucrative in Atlantic City, where the political leaders had declared that it was a "wide-open town" well before Prohibition. C. Winder and Son had a well-known Northside delivery service. However, by the time this photograph was taken in the 1930s, the concession had been sold to a Mr. Perry. (ACFPL.)

Decades before airplanes trailed banners pitching suntan lotion to beachfront crowds, enterprising sailors leased their sail space for advertising and plied the waters off Atlantic City's beach. In 1935, the *Mascotte*, seen here, managed two very different sponsors. (ACFPL.)

TIMES OF CHANGE

The war effort was widespread even before the troops began converging on the city. Women war workers at S. G. Seyfang Laboratories put the finishing touches on three of the many reconnaissance balloons made in Atlantic City to further the war effort. (ACFPL.)

Sailors, sometimes not known for precision marching, were in impeccable cadence on Atlantic Avenue in a military review. Note the crowds of spectators lining the boardwalk in the rear and the ramps leading to the walk. (ACFPL.)

This might have been Iwo Jima, Guadalcanal, or Saipan. Indeed, some who stormed the beach here at Atlantic City eventually went ashore on such distant sands. Boardwalk crowds gathered to watch the mock assaults, complete with exploding bombs and the rattling of machine guns. (ACFPL.)

First Lady Eleanor Roosevelt (center, in the flowered dress) came to Atlantic City to encourage the Red Cross and other volunteers as well as to visit some of the thousands of soldiers at the Thomas L. England hospital for injured servicemen. (ACFPL.)

Recognizing the constant need for blood at the T. L. English Hospital, healthy soldiers streamed to the blood donation center in one of the hotels. It was a chance to help the war effort and an opportunity for soldiers to see a pretty young nurse up close. (ACFPL.)

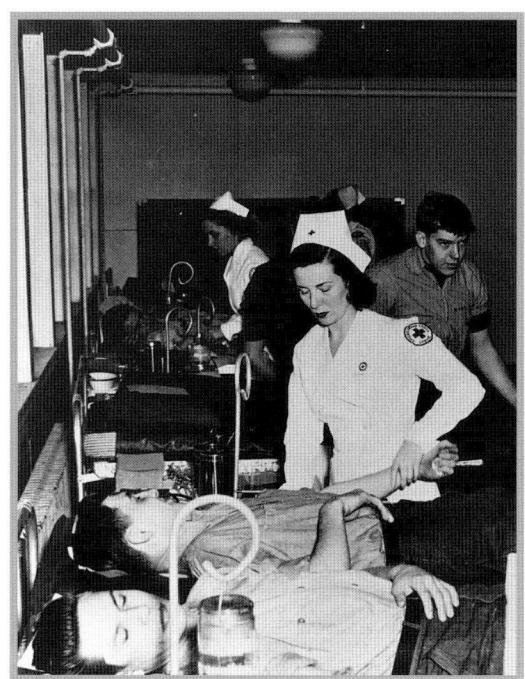

This handsome veteran, Jimmy Wilson, had known so much of war that he had lost both arms and both legs. Yet in the midst of enough adversity to kill most men's spirit, he met, wooed, and married a lovely young woman, Bea Hilsec. They danced at their wedding in an Atlantic City hotel ballroom. Quite naturally, they honeymooned in the city. (ACFPL.)

The hurricane of 1944 unleashed its fury on Atlantic City, wrecking portions of the world-famous boardwalk and Steel Pier. The hurricane also destroyed the H. J. Heinz Pier beyond reconstruction. (ACFPL.)

The September 14, 1944, hurricane wrecked the H. J. Heinz Pier and removed a section of Steel Pier. Then, in March 1962, a nor'easter tore up blocks of sidewalks and streets, submerging almost every ground-floor establishment in Atlantic City in water and sand. The city needed more than a year to clean up and repair the damage. The storm destroyed more of the city than another storm in March 1984 and Hurricane Gloria on September 26, 1985. (ACFPL.)

By 1946, wide Atlantic Avenue was a mix of automobiles and streetcars. The double-tracked streetcar line occupied the middle of the street, and even with street parking for automobiles there was ample room to keep all traffic moving smoothly. (ACFPL.)

The piers attracted many amusements. With a relaxed attitude toward liquor during Prohibition and toward gambling before the casinos, the city also prized its fights and fighters. Even in the twilight of his career, after World War II, Joe Louis, shown in trunks on the left, drew thousands to the boardwalk for training sessions and bouts. (ACFPL.)

During the Congress Hotel fire of January 7, 1952, more than 40 pieces of modern equipment could not save the blocks bounded by the boardwalk, St. Charles Place, States Avenue, and New Jersey Avenue. Some 400 firefighters from 17 municipalities battled freezing temperatures to stop its spread. Winds gusting more than 40 miles per hour lofted flaming debris across streets and spread the fire to smaller buildings, as seen here. (ACFPL.)

The intense heat of the Congress Hotel fire of 1952 set other buildings afire. Firefighters saved the Breakers Hotel by cooling it with their hoses; the hot bricks turned the water into steam. No one died in the fire, as businesses were closed for the season. However, the fire consumed four hotels, the Globe Theater, three stores, a fire truck, and 10 guesthouses. Twelve other buildings also suffered damage. (ACFPL.)

The boardwalk at Park Place, shown in 1955, was famous even before Charles Darrow's Monopoly game made its real estate the game's costliest properties. Bounded on the south by a tiny street named Park Place, Brighton Park, at right, was an 1879 gift to the city by the owner of the Brighton Hotel and a Philadelphia saw maker. The grand Traymore and Marlborough-Blenheim hotels were just a few yards beyond. An unemployed heating contractor when he invented Monopoly in 1930, Charles Darrow created the 20th century's best-selling game and earned a plaque at boardwalk and Park Place for immortalizing Atlantic City's streets and landmarks. (Conectiv.)

TOWARD THE MODERN ERA

On the eve of the city's transformation into a land of glittering casino buildings, the boardwalk and its hotels were proclaimed as emblems of family entertainment—a city of Sunday morning bicycling in front of the boardwalk hotels, including the imposing Traymore. This 1958 picture of serenity would soon disappear to make room for the huge hotel-casino complexes that would rise after gambling was legalized in Atlantic City in 1976. (ACFPL.)

In its early days, the Atlantic City beach admitted all sorts of recreation. Note the horseback riders in the surf in this July 1890 illustration from *Harper's Weekly*. The woman in the wheelchair demonstrates that the city's alleged health benefits attracted visitors for decades after the city's founding. (Ruffolo.)

OPPOSITE: Horseback riding lasted into the 1960s and beyond. It was eventually restricted to the off-season months. (ACFPL.)

The front of Convention Hall, as it looked in 1960, has changed little since the day it opened. Millions of conventioneers have passed through the big front doors. Inside, the main hall can be converted from a huge exhibit area to a concert hall seating 20,000 to 30,000 people. Pres. Lyndon B. Johnson was nominated here in 1964 in his campaign to be president. (ACFPL.)

No matter what the measurement—size of crowd, demand for tickets, or audience enthusiasm—nothing came close to matching the accord given the Beatles when they came to Convention Hall in 1964. With joy bordering on agony, a Beetles fan wept and emoted as the concert progressed. She became mesmerized by the vibrant harmonies of the group until, midway through the concert, she collapsed. (ACFPL.)

OPPOSITE: The serious young men from Liverpool first enchanted the press in the afternoon, then in the evening enthralled one of the largest crowds ever to jam into the hall. (ACFPL.)

When bathers in 1962 grew tired of the sea and its shifting moods, they could admire the Atlantic City skyline from the beach. The grand hotels were stone and brick monuments that replaced scores of picturesque wooden structures from 1910 through the early 1930s. Whether wood or stone, the hotels coaxed the well-heeled off the beach and into an experience modeled on European resorts. (Conectiv.)

Sand sculpture was banned for years after 1944 when a number of sand artists were unmasked as con artists. The attraction to the sculpture is easy to understand, especially for this youngster digging on the Atlantic City beach in 1975. (ACFPL.)

Dreams have always been Atlantic City's long suit. However, as both city residents and tourists awaited the results of the statewide approval of gambling casinos in 1976, dreams verged on nightmares. The city would change dramatically; to students of architecture and tradition this meant some (if not most) of the imposing boardwalk structures would disappear. Many wondered what possibly might replace the past. Boardwalk denizens watched the Hotel Traymore as it was prepared for demolition, sighing over the imminent demise of the fine old hotel. (ACFPL.)

The final blows to the Traymore were swift and awesome. Artfully placed dynamite sliced away the facades of the familiar twin towers, opposite. Then, huge caches of explosives leveled in seconds what had taken three-quarters of a century to build. The Traymore had vanished and so had much of the city's past. (ACFPL.)

And so today and tomorrow dawn, and the city awaits the appraisal and approval of new generations. The city is transformed as far as buildings are concerned, but on any sunny afternoon in summertime, crowds of tourists stroll the unique boardwalk. There is ample room to dream. (ACFPL.)

Arcadia Publishing is the leading local history publisher in the United States. With more than 3,000 titles in print and hundreds of new titles released every year, Arcadia has extensive specialized experience chronicling the history of communities and celebrating America's hidden stories, bringing to life people, places, and events from the past. To discover the history of other communities across the nation, please visit:

www.arcadiapublishing.com

Customized search tools allow you to find regional history books about the town where you grew up, the cities where your friends and relatives live, the town where your parents met, or even that retirement spot you've been dreaming of. The Arcadia website also provides history lovers with exclusive deals, advanced notice of new titles, e-mail alerts of author events, and much more.